STEPS TO START AND MAXIMIZE YOUR BUSINESS

A Guide to Starting Your Own Business or Maximizing Your Already Developed Business

By

John James McDonald

Owner of Brothers All Around Service LLC

© Copyright 2019 by John James McDonald

STEPS TO START AND MAXIMIZE YOUR BUSINESS

A Guide to Starting Your Own Business or Maximizing Your Already Developed Business

All rights reserved. It is not legal to reproduce, duplicate, or transmit any part of this document in either electronic means or printed format. Recording of this publication is strictly prohibited.

Dedication

Louis Cw Linsley

      Thank you for pushing me to accomplish particular dreams of mine and helping to mold me into the best version of myself. This kernel popped!

Table of Contents

Introduction	1
PART I: Starting Your Business	3
Chapter One: Do Your Research	5
Chapter Two: Basic Needs	12
Chapter Three: Leadership	36
PART II: Maximizing Your Business	40
Chapter Four: Cutting Cost, Maximizing Profit	41
Chapter Five: Engage with Customers/Clients	46
Chapter Six: Stay Organized	52
Chapter Seven: Client Communications	56
Chapter Eight: Promoting Your Business	60
Epilogue/Conclusion	79
Acknowledgments	81
About the Author	82

Introduction

First, I want to congratulate you on purchasing this book and taking the first steps into building your own legacy. I know that this can be an exciting and confusing time for you. I was in the same position once before.

This book is about starting your own business and maximizing it to its fullest potential. It will provide you with insight and tips I myself, and other successful people have used throughout our careers to build the best businesses we can. It will also provide you with the knowledge to know how to get started.

My hope for this book is that it will solve the issue you are facing. Which is starting your business or growing your already developed business. This book will highlight where you need to begin if you are starting from scratch. It will provide the basics of doing so and what some things you may need are. For established businesses, it will help you maximize profitability and deliver better service and products.

I have been in management ever since I was fifteen years old. I started off at McDonald's and I have to say, they taught me so much. From how to manage people, to dealing with problematic customers and providing a service to people. From there I was able to grow my role within other organizations and eventually run multiple million-dollar companies for other people. Before I decided to start my own company and live a life my family and I can be proud of.

Some benefits from buying this book are the knowledge you will receive from people who have implemented these exact ideas, confidence to start this new chapter of your life, insights of how to build a successful company and be a place that people want to come to and work for.

These tips and insights you are going to read about have helped hundreds of people that I have personally trained and developed. It allowed them to understand the business models and become great leaders whether they have started their own business or continued to work for someone else.

You are not going to want to wait too long to begin after reading this. Once you finish the book, start the new chapter of your life as soon as possible. This way you can get yourself on the path to greatness and build the life you can be proud of. I challenge you to do so!

PART I: Starting Your Own Business

Did you know in the United States, there are more than 28 million small business, making up a whopping 99 percent of all U.S. businesses, according to the Small Business Administration? Think about some of the most common reasons to start a business, including having an interesting business idea, designing a career that has the capability to grow with you, working toward financial freedom, or investing in yourself and your legacy, it's no wonder that there is a plethora of small businesses.

However, not every small business will be successful. In fact, only about thirty three percent of businesses with employees survive two years, and about half survive five years. So, you may be in for a real challenge when you decide to take the plunge, ditch your day job, and become a business owner. The stage is often set in the beginning, so making sure you follow all of the necessary steps when starting your business will build the foundation for success.

Hopefully, this book will stack the odds in your favor and you'll be able to beat those statistics. Take your time, take notes and treat this as your "bible". Remember, that the only limitations you have, are the ones you say you have. Every part of your life had a beginning and more than likely you didn't know how or where to start, but you got it done. For this part, it is time to simplify.

"WAKE UP WITH DETERMINATION, GO TO BED WITH SATISFACTION"

Success.com

Chapter One: Research

Hopefully at this point you have a business idea. If not, that's okay. Take some time to figure out your strengths and the unique type of business you want. But, let's take some time to balance your idea with a little reality. Does your idea have the capability to succeed? Are you going to need to run your business idea through a validation process before you go any further?

For a small business to be successful, it needs to solve a problem, fulfill a need or offer something the market wants.

There are a number of ways you can identify this need, including research, focus groups, and even trial and error. As you research and explore the market, some of the questions you should answer include:

Is there a need for your anticipated products/services?

Who needs it?

Are there other companies offering similar products/services now?

What is the competition like?

How will your business fit into the market?

You'll also need to consider the main things that you are going to need. Let's discuss and identify the possible needs you may have to make sure you are set up for success.

Deciding to be an LLC, Sole Proprietorship, Partnership, Corporation or Cooperative.

There are differences in each one and each has their own benefits and drawbacks. It is important to decide which best fits your needs.

Sole Proprietorship

A sole proprietorship is a business owned by only one person. It is easy to set-up and is the least costly among all forms of ownership. However, the owner faces unlimited liability; meaning, the creditors of the business may go after the personal assets of the owner if the business cannot pay them. The sole proprietorship form is one of the most commonly adopted forms by small business entities.

Partnership

A partnership is a business owned by two or more persons who contribute resources into the entity. The partners divide the profits of the business among themselves. In general partnerships, all partners have unlimited liability. In limited partnerships, creditors cannot go after the personal assets of the limited partners.

Corporation

A corporation is a business organization that has a separate legal personality from its owners. Ownership in a stock corporation is represented by shares of stock. The owners (stockholders) enjoy limited liability but have limited involvement in the company's operations. The board of directors, an elected group from the stockholders, controls the activities of the corporation. In addition to those basic forms of business ownership, these are some other types of organizations that are common today:

Limited Liability Company

Limited liability companies (LLC) in the USA, are hybrid forms of business that have characteristics of both a corporation and a partnership. An LLC is not incorporated; hence, it is not considered a corporation. Nevertheless, the owners enjoy limited liability like in a corporation. An LLC may elect to be taxed as a sole proprietorship, a partnership, or a corporation. This is the most commonly adopted form for small businesses.

Cooperative

A cooperative is a business organization owned by a group of individuals and is operated for their mutual benefit. The persons making up the group are called members. Cooperatives may be incorporated or unincorporated. Some examples of cooperatives are water and electricity (utility) cooperatives, cooperative banking, credit unions, and housing cooperatives. This more than likely will not apply to you. But, for information purposes, I listed it.

Pick and Register Your Business Name

Your business name plays a role in almost every aspect of your business, you are going to want it to be a good one. Make sure you think through all the potential implications as you explore your options and choose your business name.

Once you have chosen a name for your business, you will need to check if it's trademarked or currently in use. Then, you will need to register it. A sole proprietor must register their business name with either their state or county clerk. Corporations, LLCs, or limited partnerships typically register their business name when the formation paperwork is filed. A quick google search for your state will show you how to file your name and pay the fees. Also, check to see if your state offers anything for active military or veterans. In Pennsylvania, active military or veterans can file their business for free. You can also hire a company such as LegalZoom to help file. They do charge, and I don't believe it is necessary for you to do so.

Don't forget to register your domain name once you have selected your business name. Try these options if your ideal domain name is taken. You'll want this for when you go to design your website if you choose to do so. I highly recommend you have a website. We will discuss the benefits of that shortly.

Licenses, Permits and Insurance (if applicable)

Paperwork is a part of the process when you start your own business. There are a variety of small business licenses and permits that may apply to your situation, depending on the type of business you are starting and where you are located. You will need to research what licenses and permits apply to your business during the start-up process. Insurance is something you will want to make sure you get quickly. Many customers won't consider you as legitimate without being insured. Also, you do not want to risk something going wrong and your company being sued. It could shut you down and your hard work will be wasted. Cover your business as you do your home/car. It is well worth the expense.

Building Your Website

A website is one of the most important things for your business. One it helps show that you are legitimate and serious. But, it also lets you connect with your customers. Living in the digital world, a website is now a necessity for a business, albeit big or small. If you have a business and don't have a website, I can almost guarantee that you are losing a number of great opportunities for your business. A website itself can be used to accomplish many different marketing strategies to help your business grow. The web has a far wider reach than any other form of advertising. While it takes time to build up enough traffic to your website to make a worthwhile impact on your company's marketing campaign, it costs next to nothing to do so. Your website will be the center of your company's online presence; through it, you advertise your business around the Web on social media sites, forums and through pay-per-click advertising programs.

Increasing visibility is one major factor that makes having a website important. Even if people have heard about your company, they may want to carry out research online first, before entertaining the idea of leaving the comfort of their own home or hiring you to perform a service. If you have a physical office or business location, websites usually provide a map and directions to the company's shops or offices, for visitors to less likely have trouble finding your location.

Another important reason why having a website to represent your business is to give you credibility. By building a website, you are giving your business the opportunity to tell consumers why they should trust you and the testimonials and facts to back up those opportunities. Believe it or not, most people will search the internet for a product or service before they purchase to check the credibility first. When you provide good service or product, positive word-of-mouth about your business is likely to spread. Which in turn, delivers more repeat and new business. A website will not only give you credibility, but it will also help to give the impression that your company is bigger and more successful than it may actually be. One of the great things about the internet is that the size of your company does not really matter. There is no reason that you can't get your site to rank in Google ahead of a large multinational competitor and funnel off some of their traffic. This is a big part of the reason that a website is even more important for a small business than a big one, it tends to level the playing field. You'll want to make sure you use effective keywords for your SEO (search engine optimizer).

There are several different options you can use for building a website. Wix is a free website builder that is online. They will even give you a free domain name. I recommend that you upgrade to their premium account however. The reason for this is that their free website uses a generic domain for you and they advertise like crazy on your webpage. It is not very professional looking, in my opinion. I have tried out a few different website builders, Wix in my opinion was the easiest and best to use.

You also have the option of paying someone to build you a site, register the domain and optimize the SEO for you. This route generally allows you to rank quicker on Google and other search engines. But, it can be very costly. So, choose wisely. Remember, the more you do on your own, the more you save and the more you learn. This is also developing more skills.

> "Sometimes Later Becomes Never. Do it Now"!
>
> Success.com

Chapter Summary/Key Takeaways

- Do research, see what your state requires you to have to operate your business.
- Pick your business structure, take time and make sure it is the appropriate fit for you.
- Register your business name and domain. Needed for your website!

In this next Chapter, we will go over Accounting, Point of Sales Systems, Business Banking, Capital, Recruiting, and Location.

"PUSH YOURSELF, BECAUSE NO ONE ELSE IS GOING TO DO IT FOR YOU"

Success.com

Chapter Two: Basic Needs

Now that we have gone over formalities to start the actual business. Let's go over the businesses basic needs to operate. As previously mentioned, we will cover Accounting, Point of Sales Systems, Business Banking, Capital, Recruiting, and Location.

Accounting System

Small businesses run most effectively when there are systems in place. One of the most important systems for a small business is an accounting system.

Your accounting system is necessary in order to create and manage your budget, set your rates and prices, conduct business with others, and file your taxes. You can set up your accounting system yourself or hire an accountant to take away some of the guesswork. If you decide to get started on your own, make sure you consider these questions that are vital when choosing accounting software.

Which Accounting Software Features Do You Need? Eliminate accounting software choices by making a list of the small business accounting features you need to run your business. Most of the small business accounting features include:

Inventory management

Sales tracking

Manage customer contacts or work with your current contact management software

Merchant account support to accept credit card payments

Budgeting

Estimates

Payroll

Business tax reporting

Industry-Specific Accounting Software

Some accounting software is designed specifically for industries such as manufacturing, and wholesale distributors. If your small business is in an industry with specific accounting requirements, there may be particular accounting software with features to meet those requirements. Make sure you inquire about these possibilities.

Talk to Others About Accounting Software

Before you buy accounting software, talk to at least three other people who use accounting software in businesses that are similar to yours. Discuss what they like about their accounting software and what needs improvement. You may find that there is no perfect accounting software out there, but do not be discouraged. Your goal is to find accounting software that best meets your small business needs.

Other Accounting Software Considerations

Since you have narrowed down your accounting software choices keep this list of questions with you while you shop for small business accounting software.

1. Will the Accounting Software Grow with Your Business?

    A. Find out if the software has modules you can add later if needed. A module that is commonly added after a business grows is for payroll accounting.

    B. If modules or features cannot be added, does the software upgrade easily to a more capable version of the same accounting software? Or, does the software export to a data format such as CSV so it can be read by should you switch to another accounting software title later?

2. What Accounting Software Supports Your Bank Support?

   A. Being able to download transactions from your bank saves a lot of time, so find out what accounting software your bank works with. Check with your bank as the may have some software or a device you can purchase. More on this later.

3. Online or Desktop Accounting Software?

   A. Online accounting software is web-based software that runs securely through an Internet browser. Online accounting software is especially convenient for accessing accounting data and records from multiple computers.

4. Can Access Be Restricted for Some Users?

   A. If more than one person is using the accounting software, one individual may need full access to all functions, but others may only need access to data entry areas and not reports.

5. Does the Accounting Software Come with a Free Trial?

   A. It is always best if you can try the software before you buy it. To see how useful the software documentation is, click on Help in the free trial, then look for a user guide or tutorials. There are free services out there for accounting purposes such as QuickBooks.

Accounting Software Support Options

Remember to figure support costs into your accounting software budget. Some accounting software provides fee-based support by email

14

or phone from the moment you start using the software. However, it is common for the cost of small business accounting software to provide support at no cost for a set period, so you can ask questions when you first start using the software without incurring additional expenses. After that time, you pay for support annually, quarterly or on a per-use basis.

The accounting software may have a free online user forum where you can ask questions as well. It is often a good option to fee-based support when your question is about how to use a feature.

Don't Pay for Features You Are Not Going to Use

A small, less complex business will probably need fewer features than a larger business would. Remember the question in Step 3 regarding upgrading or adding modules to the accounting software later? No matter how irresistible extra "bells and whistles" seem, resist the temptation to buy more accounting software than you need.

Generally, you pay more for more features in accounting software and if your business grows enough to need more robust financial features, the cost is justified. For smaller businesses, there are now enough accounting software options available that over-buying is unnecessary.

Accountant or Accounting Software?

Accounting software does not replace an accountant for ensuring that your business adheres to legal and accepted accounting and tax practices. But, when you use accounting software, you take every day accounting tasks out of the hands of an accountant, which saves money for a small business. When first starting out, every penny saved is a penny earned.

Also, good accounting software will have the reports you need to give to your accountant on a monthly, quarterly and annual basis.

Either the reports can be printed, or they can be delivered securely to an accountant electronically. Make sure you ask your accountant what reports are needed and be sure you can generate them with the accounting software you are considering.

Point of Sale System

A point of sale system (POS) is something you will want to look into getting. There are a lot of options out there for you to choose from. Some of those options are Square, Clever, PayPal or even one your Business Bank may offer (More on this one later).

For my business I use Square. Depending on what exactly your business is going to be doing, (lawn care, restaurant, consulting) you may need a physical system attached to a tablet or computer, or you may just need a card reader that attaches to your phone. I use Square because they offer the card reader for free. You can buy the full POS for a computer with them as well. Their support is solid as well.

You will want to really think about exactly what you need for this type of system. Again, when you are starting out, every penny saved is a penny earned. So, it may be beneficial for you to choose the system that is basic and free. They make their money by charging you a percentage each time a card is swiped. So, you may also want to consider charging an additional fee to cover the cost that is charged to you.

Business Banking

This is a crucial component of your business. This is where you are going to store your money. It is critical that you take your time selecting your bank. Don't just use the same bank your personal checking and savings sit in. They may not offer the best deals for your business needs.

Do an internet search to see what banks may offer a free business checking account, no limits or fees or only implement fees after "x" amount of transactions. There are a lot of options for banks, albeit an online bank or a brick and mortar bank. I live in Pennsylvania and here Citizens Bank offers free business checking, with no minimum to open the account and no fees for the first one hundred transactions. When I first started out, this was very important as I did not have any capital other than my own personal savings. So, I needed to limit spending as much as possible.

Also, look and see if your bank offers a POS system or something to help you with your sales. This will ensure that there are no issues there when it comes time to get your money,

Business Location

Setting up your place of business is important for the operation of your business, whether you will have a home office, a shared or private office space, or a retail location.

You will need to think about your location, equipment, and overall setup, and make sure your business location works for the type of business you will be doing. You will also need to consider if it makes more sense to buy or lease your commercial space.

Working from home offers many advantages including the flexibility of setting your own schedule, saving time, and gas money by eliminating your daily commute. However, being successful in a home office requires creating an office space that promotes efficiency in a non-traditional work environment. Consider the following tips to help define a professional working space for your new business.

Home-based

More and more retail businesses are getting a start at home. Some may eventually move to a commercial store location, while many remain in the business owner's spare room. This type of location is an inexpensive option, but growth may be limited. It is harder to separate business and personal life in this setup, and the retailer may run into problems if there isn't a different address and/or phone number for the business.

Office Needs

Before claiming a corner in one of your rooms and calling it an office, make a detailed list of your most basic needs for a home office or a "critical needs" list. Your needs list should include a desk, computer, printer, and telephone.

If you are a comic book designer, for example, you may need both a small desk for your computer and a larger table or workspace for your artwork.

However, if you are a consultant, you may need additional space for several locking, fireproof file cabinets, and possibly space for clients to meet with you. When making your list of critical needs, it is important to think about how you plan to use the home office.

Pick an Area for Your Home Office Space

Once you have made your critical needs list, you'll have a better idea of how much space you need for the office and can set aside a dedicated area of your home. Make sure it is in a quiet area with some privacy. This is especially important if you share the house with a spouse, children, or even a roommate.

For example, if you have a spare room with a door it may be best because it can help limit noise from the rest of the house. If you are on the phone often, you'll appreciate that. Or, if you'll be meeting with clients in your home office, it may be more efficient to choose a room near the front entrance of the house.

Workspace and Storage Requirements

Quite often, a home-based office has a limited amount of space and can feel cramped even with only a chair and desk in the room. However, maintaining a professional office is dependent upon good organization (more later). That means having a space that has plenty of room for both storage (supplies) and a big enough work area. You may have to get creative.

A rule of thumb is that any files or supplies that you use frequently should be easily accessible. Again, the goal is to create an organized office space that meets all of your basic needs and allows you to function efficiently.

Lighting

If you are able to, choose a space for your office that allows plenty of natural light. You can also enhance the area with direct lighting. Start by providing general, overhead lights that fill most of the work area. Regardless of the type of lighting available, make sure that your computer is positioned so that it prevents glare. The object is to create lighting that minimizes eye strain.

Dedicated Phone for Your Home Business

One of the many benefits of working from home is having reduced overhead. However, the initial savings from sharing a phone line with your home and business can ultimately cost you. A home phone is less professional and may allow clients to question the legitimacy of the business.

One of the downfalls of using a home phone is having to share voicemail that uses a message from both family and business. It confuses customers. Likewise, when sharing a phone, you risk having a child or other family member answers the phone, giving the impression that you are not running a real business. It is best to use a dedicated phone line for your home office. Of course, this can include using a cell phone, or a VoIP (Internet-based) phone.

Invest in the Right Home Office Equipment

Getting started in your home office by using the right equipment is essential, and phones are not the only must-have pieces of equipment. Unfortunately, it can be tempting to skimp on key equipment and splurge on unnecessary items, such as office decor.

Money should be spent on a good desk with proper workspace, a comfortable chair that can provide back support, a computer with efficient memory and performance, a fast Internet connection, and any other specialized equipment, tools, or software that is key for performance in your area of expertise.

Separate Professional from Personal

When working from home, it is important to keep your personal life from entering your business life and the opposite is the same. Setting up a business bank account is the first step in helping you avoid mixing personal expenses with your business expenses (more later).

To also reduce confusion, try to store personal checks, records, and even mail in a room separate from your office. Fully segregating these may also help when it comes time to file taxes.

Tax deductions related to home offices are increasingly scrutinized, and the more you can prove that the office is a separate and dedicated area, the better chance of meeting IRS definitions of a home office.

Use Formal Processes and Procedures in Your Office

You won't need to write a formal employee handbook or publish a list of office rules but determining a formal system of operations for your home office is useful.

A handbook should include everything from a guide to record-keeping and paying invoices to logging time with customers and mileage for business trips. Keeping formal procedures in place for standard business functions will ensure your office stays organized, and that information is available when you need it.

Establish Office Hours

Flexibility is a benefit of working for yourself in your home, but it still requires that you put in a fair amount of time. Setting a typical schedule for working in your office will help you stay focused. Perhaps even more important, keeping standard office hours (for the most part) also helps your clients know when you are available.

After all, you might do most of your creative work in the middle of the night, but your clients are likely to keep more traditional work hours. As a result, you'll need to make yourself available during the hours that your clients are at work. Establishing office hours can also help minimize distractions, and unannounced calls, or drop-in visits from well-meaning friends and family.

Have a Clock

Once your office hours are set, don't forget to hang a clock on a wall or place one on your desk. While this may seem laughable and obvious, the truth is that when working from home, it's easy to forget about time. Before you know it, you have worked a sixteen-hour day, for the fourth day in a row. Even though your work is at home, you still need to close the door at some point and say enough is enough for the day.

Retail Location Options

Think about the businesses that are in your area. They can range from being a house to a skyscraper type of building. Listed below are some additional options for your business needs.

Mall Space

From kiosks to large stores, a mall has many companies competing under one roof. In a mall, there are generally 3 to 5 anchor stores or large chain stores and dozens of smaller retail shops. Because of the high amount of customer traffic malls generate, the rent is much higher than other retail locations.

Before selecting this type of store location, be sure the mall shopper demographic matches that of your customers. Mall retailers will have to make some sacrifices in independence and adhere to a set of rules stipulated by mall management.

Shopping Center

Strip malls and other attached, adjoining retail locations will also have guidelines or rules for how they prefer their tenants to do business. These rules are probably more lenient than a mall, but make sure you can live with them before signing a lease. Your community probably has many shopping centers of various sizes.

Some shopping centers may have as few as three units or as many as twenty. The types of retailers and the product or services they offer will also vary. One thing you definitely want to investigate before choosing this type of store location is parking. Some shopping centers have a limited parking area for your customers.

Downtown

Like the mall, this type of store location may be another premium choice. However, there may be more freedom and fewer rules for the business owner. Many communities are hard at work to revitalize their downtown areas, and retailers can greatly benefit from this effort. However, the lack of parking is generally a big issue for downtown retailers. You'll find many older, well-established specialty stores in a downtown area.

Free Standing Locations

This type of retail location is basically any stand-alone building. It can be tucked away in a neighborhood location or right off a busy highway. Depending on the landlord, there are generally no restrictions on how a retailer should operate his business.

It will probably have ample parking and the cost per square foot will be reasonable. The price for all that freedom may be traffic. Unlike the attached retail locations, where customers may wander in because they were shopping nearby, the retailer of a free-standing location must work at marketing to get the customer inside.

Office Building

The business park or office building may be another option for a retailer, especially when they cater to other businesses. Tenants share maintenance costs and the image of the building is usually upscale and professional.

Virtual Office

Another option here is a virtual office. A quick internet search can help you locate offices in your area that offer these services. These virtual offices have a few benefits for new businesses or businesses that primarily run from home.

Typically, there are packages that you can purchase. A base package may look something like just the physical address and mail service. Whereas a middle range package may include the lower tier as well as phone number and answering service. High tier may include the preceding two and also allow you a few days of actual office space use and unlimited access to the conference room and lounge area. This is a great option for people who don't want to have their home address listed for the business.

Buying or Leasing A Building

If your business has become successful and your current situation or building no longer fits your needs, you may want to consider either buying a commercial building or leasing a bigger one.

Pros of Buying a Business Property

There are a few benefits to buying a business property. Some of those benefits are:

Low Financing Costs

With current interest rates at historic lows you can take advantage of low mortgage rates to own your own premises, thereby building ownership equity rather than paying a landlord.

Fixed Overhead

Owning your own building means that you know what your future costs will be. Mortgage rates have been declining for decades and do not fluctuate like lease costs sometimes do. By owning the property, you know that the overhead is fixed for the mortgage period. On the other hand, lease costs are affected by improvements to the building, changing real estate values, demand, and other factors. When leasing business property, there is no guarantee that at the end of a lease period you will be able to renew your lease under similar terms. Recently, for instance, A local McDonald's located in a nearby mall, was given a choice to either do a million-dollar renovation and only sign a one-year lease or leave. They closed as the amount of money was to much for that short of a lease agreement.

Stability

If your business uses specialized equipment, machinery, or fixtures that are difficult and/or expensive to move, or if the business requires extensive renovations, ownership of the premises may be preferable. Otherwise, if the landlord does not renew your lease when it expires you could be facing extensive costs, particularly if the lease stipulates that you must return the premises to the original condition when you leave.

Appreciation in Value

If you can purchase a building in an upcoming area and/or at the bottom of a real estate cycle, the property may greatly increase in value in the future. This is not guaranteed, but it is a possibility.

Collateral

Premises owned by the business are an asset that can be used as collateral for a debt or equity financing.

Freedom from Landlords

Not all landlords are created equal, and some landlords are prone to cutting costs by neglecting maintenance, security, and capital improvements.

Leasing for Additional Revenue

If you buy a business property and there is extra space on the premises you may be to bring in additional revenue by subletting (See 5 Ways Your Business Can Make More Money.) This can be lucrative provided there is a steady demand for space in your location and a good supply of quality tenants. However, as anyone who has ever been a landlord can tell you, dealing with tenants can be very frustrating and time-consuming, and in a slowing economy, this tends to be more of a problem.

Disadvantages of Buying a Business Property

There are some cons to owning a business property though. Owning is not always feasible for companies or individuals and it can cause more issues. Some of these issues are:

Possible Decline in Property Value

If after a number of years in a particular location it becomes necessary to move, owning your own commercial space can be a major drawback. Deteriorating business conditions, changes in the neighborhood, or local tax increases may cause a decline in value and make selling your business property very difficult.

Tying Up Capital

If your business is in a startup or growth phase you may prefer to invest capital in the business rather than buying commercial space.

Fluctuating Interest Rates

With interest rates at historic lows, an eventual rise is likely, meaning your mortgage costs may increase in future.

Cost Savings Maybe Negligible

When leasing business property, the costs of property taxes, maintenance, and repairs, security, parking, insurance, etc. are generally included in a lease agreement. If you purchase a property these expenses become your responsibility. Any decision to buy or rent should include a side by side comparison of the cost of renting versus owning. If you intend to purchase you should have an annual maintenance budget that includes money set aside for major repairs such as roof replacement, building envelope refurbishing, etc. The renewal of an existing lease can work in your favor in periods of slow demand and low occupancy rates. In such an environment if you have a good relationship with the landlord you may be able to negotiate better lease terms such as a lower rate, a longer lease period, or improvements to the premises.

Do you really want to be a landlord? Your accountant can analyze your operating budgets, investigate tax issues and advise on the pros and cons of buying versus renting from a financial perspective, but when making the decision to buy you should also take into consideration how much extra time will be taken up by being an owner/landlord. Dealing with maintenance issues and tenants (if subletting) can consume a great deal of time that may be better spent focusing on your own business activities.

Is your business growing or declining? Owning a business property can be problematic if your business is in growth or a downsize phase where you may need to sell the existing premises to either acquire additional space or reduce your space requirements. Renegotiating a lease is much less difficult.

Business Plan

You need a plan to make your business idea a reality. A business plan is a structure that will guide your business from the start-up phase through establishment and eventually business growth. While not a complete necessity, I highly recommend you have one.

The good news is that there are different types of business plans for different types of businesses.

If you intend to seek money from an investor or financial institution, a traditional business plan will be needed. This type of business plan is generally long and thorough and has a common set of sections that investors and banks look for when they are validating your idea.

If you don't anticipate seeking financial support, a simple one-page business plan can give you clarity about what you hope to achieve and how you plan to do it. In fact, you can even create a working business plan on the back of a napkin and improve it over time. A plan in writing is always better than nothing. Traditional business plans have a few elements and a specific structure to how it should be laid out.

The executive summary is the first section of your small business plan in which you'll probably write last. This section highlights at least one important statement from each of the other sections in your business plan, while also including basic information about your business such as your business name and location, description of your business and its products and/or services, your management team and mission statement.

The company description section of your business plan is typically the second section. The company description outlines vital details about your company, such as where you are located, how large the company is, what you do and what you hope to accomplish. This section also describes the vision and direction of the company so potential lenders and partners can develop an accurate impression of who you are.

The products or services section of your business plan should clearly describe what products and/or services you're selling with an emphasis on the value you're providing to your customers or clients. This section will also include pricing information, a comparison to similar products or services in the market and an outline of future offerings.

The market analysis section of your business plan comes after the products and services section and should provide a detailed overview of the industry you intend to sell your product or service in, including statistics to support your claims. This section also includes information about the industry, target market, and competition.

The marketing strategy section of your business plan builds upon the market analysis section. This section outlines where your business fits into the market and how you will price, promote, and sell your product or service.

The management summary section of your business plan describes how your business is structured, introduces who is involved, outlines external resources, and explains how the business is managed.

The financial analysis section of your business plan should contain the details for financing your business now, what will be needed for future growth, and an estimation of your operating expenses. Take your time here, as they will focus on this section.

The appendix of your business plan includes information that supports your statements, assumptions, and reasoning used in the other sections of your business plan. This may include graphs, charts, statistics, photos, marketing materials, research, and other relevant data.

My company can design a business plan for you if needed. Visit my website at: www.brothersallaroundservice.com

Business Capital

Starting a small business doesn't have to require a lot of money, but it will involve some initial investment as well as the ability to cover ongoing expenses before you are turning a profit. Develop a spreadsheet that estimates the startup costs for your business (licenses and permits, equipment, legal fees, insurance, market research, inventory, trademarking, grand opening events, property leases, etc.), as well as what you anticipate you will need to keep your business running for at least 12 months (rent, utilities, marketing, and advertising, production, supplies, travel expenses, employee salaries, your own salary, etc.). I generally recommend between 50-75 thousand to cover these points. More or less may be needed however.

Those numbers combined is the initial investment you will need. Now that you have a rough number in mind, there are a number of ways you can fund your small business, including:

Financing

Small business loans

Small business grants

Angel investors

Crowdfunding

You can also attempt to get your business off the ground by bootstrapping, using as little capital as necessary to start your business. You may find that a combination of the paths listed above work best. The goal here, though, is to work through the options and create a plan for setting up the capital you need to get your business off the ground.

One of the most difficult parts of starting a business for many entrepreneurs is figuring out where to get the capital needed to get the business up and running. If you don't have the money saved up, can't or don't want to take out a loan, are hesitant to ask family and friends to chip in, and don't want to rack up credit card debt on start-up costs, how can you fund your business?

Believe it or not, there are financing options other than loans and credit cards for those of us working with a bootstrap budget. Explore these four options to decide which is the best way to fund your business with very little start-up capital.

Minimalist Approach

There are certain things you must spend money on when you start a business, and there's no negotiating it. Filing fees, fees for permits and licenses, and safety precautions, to name some. But, there are plenty of start-up business expenses that are much more flexible.

Think about it. Do you need brand new or the best equipment from the start, or can you get by with your existing or other pre-owned equipment? Do you need to immediately launch a direct mail campaign, or can you get started with marketing activities that require less of an investment, such as social media?

Start by making a list of all of your potential start-up costs, then come up with less costly alternatives. You may be surprised how many expenses you can cut or at least postpone until you are making some sales. And don't ignore the power of technology; there are many ways you can reduce start-up expenses in your business and do more with less by using technology.

Obtain a Partner

If you have been approaching your new business as a solo endeavor, you might want to explore expanding into a partnership. Teaming up with a colleague or friend can not only double your manpower, but it can also help you provide new and complementary products and services to your existing target market. You may even find that it helps you break into a new niche.

Before entering into a partnership, you should make sure that you take time to research your potential partner to ensure he or she is a good fit for your needs, has a positive reputation and can commit to the partnership. And make sure you work with an attorney to create a contract (operating agreement) that outlines the terms and conditions of your partnership before getting started.

Apply for a Small Business Grant

Small business grants are available from a number of resources including state governments and private groups. Although the grant application process can be a time consuming one from finding a relevant grant opportunity to conducting research into the opportunity, and specific requirements to investing the time necessary to complete and submit your application it will be well worth it if you win the award.

To get started, explore this list of small business grant programs by state. A quick internet search will be able to help identify local programs.

Crowdfund

Crowdfunding is when a business, organization or individual asks the general public for donations and monetary support for a project. Unlike peer-to-peer lending, crowdfunding is a form of microfinance that does not require repayment. Many times, the organization in question will provide other perks, such as free products or discounts, as a thank you for donations, but these terms can vary widely.

There are several different ways you can open your business or specific projects up for crowdfunding; one is through the popular website, Kickstarter. A friend of mine is the Founder and CEO of a crowd-funding company called Inventrify. He is very good and helpful. He also wants to see everyone succeed.

If these options don't work for your situation, you can explore small business loans, venture capital investors and debt financing. The most important thing to remember is to do your research so you don't end up losing time, and essentially money, by being unprepared.

Recruiting and Hiring Employee's

If you will be hiring employees, now is the time to start the process. Make sure you take the time to outline the positions you need to fill, and the job responsibilities that are part of each position. The Small Business Administration has an excellent guide to hiring your first employee that is useful for new small business owners. This will be touched on a bit more in part two chapter 4.

If you are not hiring employees, but instead use independent contractors, now is the time to work with an attorney to get your independent contractor agreement in place and start your search.

Lastly, if you are hitting the small business road alone, you may not need employees or contractors, but you will still need your own support team. This team can be comprised of a mentor, small business coach, or even your family, and serves as your go-to resource for advice, motivation, and reassurance when the road gets bumpy.

Chapter Summary/Key Takeaways

This chapter covered the basic needs your company may or may not need depending on what you are doing. Some key points are:

1. Recruiting and hiring, getting the best and keeping them.

2. Business Plan, whether it be traditional or a single page. The importance of the plan if you need to obtain capital

3. Business Capital, you are going to fund the business and the various options.

The next chapter will discuss Leadership and why it is so important for your company that you be the best leader.

Chapter Three: Leadership

Leadership is incredibly important. You can have the best products or offer an amazing service to people, but the truth of the matter is, if you are a poor leader, your business will suffer.

Leadership is something that can be taught for the most part, but you need to have a natural ability to lead others as well. There are a few books that I highly recommend you read to help you better understand. I will touch on a few things I took away from those books when I read them.

The first book is "The One Minute Manager". This book is a short read and so helpful. In short, the book has three main points. One-minute goals, one-minute praises, and one-minute reprimands. Each of these three things has an important lesson

One-minute goal setting is about being aware of what is expected from the beginning. When deciding upon the desired goal and the performance standards, you record it on a single sheet of paper. It's named that way because each goal should only take a minute to read.

With the one-minute goal, both you and the employee with have a clear definition of the task/goal from the start. This is important because you can their performance of the task periodically and see if they are achieving the target.

One-minute praising. The goal with this is to catch your people doing something right and tell them about it. If you think about your previous employers, most of the time you will remember that they would always catch someone doing something wrong or incorrectly as opposed to doing a good job.

By doing the one-minute praising you are encouraging the staff and making them feel better about themselves and what they are doing. In turn, you get more quality work from your people and a happier work environment. For exceptional results, people need to be happy and put in their best.

One-minute reprimands. The third and last key point to the book. The one-minute reprimands are supposed to be given immediately following an employee's wrongdoing. It is broken down into two parts. The first part is telling the person what they did wrong, how it makes you feel and to let it sink in with them by having a few moments of silence. The second half is for you to tell them how much you value them and their work and that you believe they are capable of doing so much. Remember though, you are criticizing the work, not the employee. Do not blame the employee, just tell them why what they did is not up to standard.

One-minute reprimands are highly effective because the feedback is immediate. They are unlike the annual reviews where you are charged for things committed several weeks or months ago. If you were being scolded for a mistake you made six months back, it would hardly make any impact on you. In comparison, if you are being scolded for a mistake you made yesterday, it will more than likely affect you.

If a mistake is pointed out as soon as it is made, it can easily be corrected. Since one mistake is pointed at one time, the people hear it seriously and your message is easily conveyed to them.

The second book I recommend you read is "The Go-Getter". This is an old book printed back in 1921. But, its message holds and proves true even today. This book motivated me to increase my productivity, take more initiative to never lose my determination. The concept behind the book draws on values such as honesty, determination, passion, and responsibility. It also teaches you that even if you are faced with an insurmountable number of obstacles. Your pure will power and desire to succeed and prove everyone else wrong will carry you through and make you successful.

Becoming a leader will take a lot of time and patience. You need to remember while it is your company, the employees are the ones that interact and generally provide the service. You want them to believe in you. I myself always made sure to do the "dirty" jobs or the most difficult. I never act like I am above anyone else. You'll see me in the bathroom scrubbing toilets with the rest of the people. When you do these things, your people will believe in you and will stick by your side. Employees don't generally leave a job because of the job, they leave because of the boss/manager/owner. Treat them with respect and understanding, but don't be a pushover.

"The Harder You Work for Something, The Greater You'll Feel When You Achieve It".

Chapter Summary/Key Takeaways

In this Chapter, we went over the basics of what you need to ensure your business runs smoothly. Those were:
- Accounting Systems, using the software or just paying an accountant.
- Business Banking, finding the right bank for your business and its needs.
- Location, the best location for the most foot traffic or easily accessible.
- Point of Sale System, using the easiest system that serves all your needs and choosing the right one.
- Business Plan, having a written plan to go to investors
- Capital, the hard money to get you going.
- Recruiting, hiring the best of the best and keeping them.

- Leadership, how to be an effective leader.

In the next part of this book, we will go over maximizing your business. This section will be beneficial to both new and established businesses alike. The upcoming chapters will hopefully give you a better understanding of where you can save and where you need to make sure that you are set up for success.

PART II: Maximizing Your Business

Business owners want their bottom line to be as profitable as possible. To increase profit, you must be diligent in cutting frivolous costs and boosting productivity among employees. This ongoing process often faces many challenges. The key to success is to focus on the end goal and always remember that the business's profits will serve two purposes. You can reinvest your profits in the business which will allow further growth and expansion, or you can take the profits as personal income in the form of a distribution.

Remember that despite your best efforts, at certain points in your business's life cycle it may not be possible to achieve the results you desire. You may run the total cost and total revenue formula and still discover that you haven't made a significant profit. Unfortunately, there are often economic factors that you have no control over which will affect your profitability. A natural disaster that affects crops or product costs or the arrival of a competitor in your area can influence your bottom line. Do not become distraught, stick to your plan and execute at the highest level possible.

I'm a firm believer that owners are in business for one reason and only one reason, and that reason is to maximize profits. Every other reason is made up of theoretical, hypothetical, make-believe, and touchy-feely thoughts that are created to make you feel good about being in charge. You want to make as much money as possible. You want to be able to take care of your employees, family, customers and offer the best services possible. This can only be done by making money and reinvesting it into the future growth of your business.

Chapter Four: Cutting Costs, Maximizing Profit

Today's business cost is higher than ever. With the need to make sure that your business is staying on top of the market and engaging customers/clients fully, many people look at a few different techniques to cut costs, but not quality. You don't want to lose any current or potential customers, right? Here are a few things you can do to cut costs and maximize your results.

Analyze and Adjust Operational Costs

A key principle of business profit is that revenue must exceed costs or expenses. So, the first step to increase profit is to analyze where the money is being spent and determine if any expenses can be trimmed or eliminated. Overhead is one of the biggest categories of expenses for almost all business owners. A long-term lease is often an effective way to manage your rent expense and hold off on annual increases. Review the other categories of expenses as well and compare them against the previous year. If there is a large increase in a specific category, be sure that you understand the reason for the changes. Perhaps you had an increase in advertising or insurance costs. If the advertising campaign is paying off in increased sales, then the higher expense may be worth it. Insurance costs are always on the rise but shop around to be sure you are getting the best rate to meet your needs.

Advertising Costs

Studies by business groups indicate that on average, small businesses typically spend approximately 5% of revenue on advertising. This figure can be substantially higher for service businesses (which are typically higher margin-oriented) or for businesses that are just starting out.

With more potential customers online than ever before, advertising does not have to be expensive. Start with building an online presence by developing a website or Facebook page. Social media is a fantastic and free way to reach people. Word a mouth is still very much dominant in today's world. Ask friends and family to spread the word about your business. You can even make ads of craigslist or another site similar to CL to direct people your way. Also, make sure you carry business cards and hand them out as much as possible. Word of Mouth is still very important and popular, especially with older generations.

Supply Costs

Now, this can vary for each company. If you are a completely online business and carry no physical products, you may just have supply costs for the devices you use. Remember you don't need to go all out on the devices, just the basic ones work very well. If you are a restaurant, you have a lot of product, you want to serve the best product as well. But, you can look for items such as cutlery, cleaning supplies and what not at much cheaper prices. Your supplier may not be giving you the best breaks. Look at stores such as Walmart or even a dollar store for certain items. Or really try to buy in bulk to maximize the savings as much as possible.

Staffing Costs

This is a relatively touchy subject. Everyone wants to make good money. I've managed a few businesses and I know first-hand employee's want to be paid well. I also know that you can really save money by maximizing your efficiency in certain areas. Look at the slow times of your business, do you have a moderate amount of people scheduled? Are you open at night and still run the same amount of people or maybe just one or two less? Check your projections and compare your sales on an hourly rate, see where you can cut an extra person. If you do services, are your people really performing to the highest level? You don't want to burn people out, but you also want to hold people accountable and make sure that they are doing what they should be.

The only thing that's real in business is maximizing profits, and the only way you are ever going to maximize profits is to find extraordinary people, treat them extraordinarily, and reward them extraordinarily for extraordinary efforts and results.

In the case of people vs. profits, or profits vs. people; you can't have one without the other, especially if you have aspirations to grow your business beyond a 1, 5, 10, 20, or 100-million-dollar Company.

You'll need to attract exceptional talent to be successful, and that means treating them extraordinarily, incentivizing and motivating them to perform, and giving them opportunities that will make them want to stay with you. Offering your people, a forward-moving career path, that will help them grow both personally and professionally, will not only create a stronger staff and dedication, but it will also maximize profit by default. So, treat them well and don't anger them with lowballing hours or cutting too much.

Benchmark Key Financials

Benchmarking your business helps you compare your costs (like rent and utilities etc.) to similar businesses in your industry to see if you are paying too much.

Once you have chosen strategies to make your business more profitable, you should prioritize them in order of importance. It's a good idea to write down your goals and the corresponding strategies to achieve them, and how you plan to implement your strategies.

Your products or services with the highest gross profit margin are the most important to your business, as they generate more money. Once you have identified your most profitable items you should concentrate on achieving higher sales targets for them. This may require you to rethink aspects of your business or to devise strategies for improvement. Consider using a business consultant to help you. The can do a lot of the legwork and help with the training and marketing of the new systems and procedures.

"DO SOMETHING TODAY THAT YOUR FUTURE SELF WILL THANK YOU FOR"

Success.com

Chapter Summary/Key Takeaways

In this chapter, we covered how to cut costs to maximize your profit. Key points are:

1. Analyze & Adjust Operational Costs
2. Advertising Costs, cheap and are very effective and cost-effective to start
3. Supply Costs, finding alternative sources or buying in bigger bulk
4. Staffing Costs, reviewing schedules and other areas to make sure time is optimized
5. Benchmark Key Financials

The next chapter will discuss how to properly engage with clients and customers in order to generate more business and better profits.

Chapter Five: Engage With Clients/Customers

The customers who are excited and engaged bring in about 25 percent more profits. However, with technology and decreasing face-to-face encounters, companies are having to find new ways to get customers excited.

Excitement is an emotion that fosters engagement. Positive experiences lead to increasing connections. Sports fans, for example, are so engaged they frequently describe their beloved team as part of their personality. This is the ultimate brand engagement.

By 2021, it is expected that customer experience/service will overtake price and product as the key brand differentiate. And yet, only about 60% of executives have a formal engagement program. Companies now must adopt a customer engagement strategy or face potentially getting left behind. Here are some ways business leaders can excite their customers in this connected digital age.

Get Feedback from Customers

Marketers must understand customers in order to excite them. Surveys can be useful if companies use proper analytics to interpret data and implement necessary changes. Get creative with surveys. Many customers will shy away from filling out a lengthy survey but will be happy to answer a single question.

Put a quick poll on social media or after an order, ask a couple of questions when following up with customers, or casually poll customers during checkout at a retail location. Use this data to make better decisions and help employees to better understand the target audience.

You will never improve your client communications if you do not ask for feedback. Routinely ask your clients how they rate their interactions with you and your company.

If you are running a medium or larger business where you don't always get to interact with your clients, consider designing a questionnaire/survey for them to complete. Or have someone designated to follow up with them.

Anytime you lose a client, especially one you have had a longstanding relationship with, you will want to do everything possible to determine what happened. Could the collapse of the relationship have something to do with anything your company could have done better with its communications?

Share What Happens Behind Closed Doors

Taking customers behind the scenes humanizes companies. This can be as simple as sharing employee stories on social media.

Disney offers "Behind the Scenes" tours to guests to engage customers in the "magic" of Disney. The tours present an unseen side of the company, demonstrating how Disney is changing the world through agriculture research or by valuing minority causes. The tours reinforce the brand while providing visitors with an immersive experience.

Launch a User Conference

A company that really understands the value of bringing users together is Harley Davidson. They have "brand-fests," which offer a place for customers to meet and create experiences that build loyalty. These experiences generate emotional connections with the brand and with other users, which leads to better brand attitudes. Brand-fests have been shown to increase sales by up to 25%.

The events should be an escape from normal life. They should flow with customers' lifestyles and opportunities for personal growth.

Package products in different ways

According to a report conducted by the American Psychological Association, first impressions form in just 39 milliseconds. Once an opinion is established, it tends to be held firmly, even when the person is presented with contradictory information. That's why the world's best brands focus on developing remarkable "unboxing" experiences.

Apple, for example, has a secret packaging room dedicated to creating an emotional experience when customers open the box. The experience feels so valuable that many of us save Apple boxes, though we toss out packaging for other products. Similar idea for a Rolex watch, plus the box is typically worth money as well.

Create a purposeful brand

Generation X and millennial's want to believe companies care about the same causes they do. A study found that while 73 percent of customers want to support companies for doing something meaningful, only 5 percent think that companies do so.

IKEA is one example of a brand that focuses on sustainability. They buy 50 percent of their wood from sustainable forests, use solar panels and control water usage in their stores. Similarly, the Seventh Generation changed the cleaning products market by developing sustainable cleaning products that cater to consumer values.

Build a contest

Contests on social media increase online audiences by as much as 34 percent and boost email sign-ups by a similar amount. While contests do not necessarily build brand loyalty in the long term, they can be an exciting way to start a relationship.

Develop a product for an under-served niche

When a company targets a small group of people, it is easier to build trust and loyalty. Niche products typically have very high-profit margins.

Tesla has operated with this strategy since its inception. They are only now starting to enter the mass market with their less expensive model. Their exclusivity has created positive feelings toward the brand for many people. Tesla is the aspiration car for today's younger generations who care both about the environment and about technological innovation.

Added value

Value is the heart of brand loyalty. Value is not about giving away free things or being the cheapest product. Instead, it is about giving customers what they want. Amazon Prime is one example. Consumers are willing to subscribe to Prime because of the added value they get in return.

Not only are items shipped to their home faster, but they receive access to cloud storage, movies, music, and world-class customer support. As a result, Amazon has been able to grow its Prime membership dramatically over the past few years.

Try something new

According to a study cited by NBC, pumpkin spice in the fall has been shown to evoke positive memories of childhood. Perhaps this is one reason why Starbucks found incredible success when they launched their pumpkin spice latte in 2003. In fact, the company could barely keep up with demand in the early days.

In some instances, luck is a meaningful component of well-timed initiatives, but so is a willingness to try new things. Starbucks took a calculated risk in introducing the pumpkin spice latte, and it paid off spectacularly. Similarly, business leaders must ensure that their organizations are daring enough to try new things.

There are a variety of ways for business leaders to develop excitement and engagement in consumers. Once the customer is the primary focus for you and your colleagues, it will be considerably easier to develop innovative approaches to creating customer excitement.

Chapter Summary/Key Takeaways

This chapter discussed how to engage with your customers. Key takeaways are:

1. Personalize each customers experience
2. Add value to your services

3. Ask customers for feedback to monitor how your company is doing and see if there is anything you need to improve on.

The next chapter will go over staying organized. It will provide you with some tips and tricks I and other coworkers use to keep focused and make the most of our time.

Chapter Six: Stay Organized

How to stay organized at work

Just a few ideas/tricks to help you stay organized at work. Because organization at work tends to carry over to your personal life as well.

1. Create digital files instead of the filing cabinets or desk drawers filled with papers. Digital is very easily accessible and can be sorted through a multitude of different ways.

2. Set reminders in your calendar on the computer or your phone. This is personally one of the easiest most helpful things that I do. Even more so because you can sync the two together so if you are away it will appear for you on your phone still. This helps to increase the organization and punctuality.

3. Accomplish one task at a time. I have been successful for a few reasons, but one is my ability to accomplish all tasks in a timely manner. I learned early on that by getting on the task completed, you get the feeling of accomplishment, which helps drive you to accomplish more tasks. I also have been successful because if a person who had more authority than me asked me to do something, I stopped what I was doing immediately and did what they needed, then went back to my task. This looks good on you as you got what they needed to be done promptly and also allowed you to achieve an accomplishment.

4. Use applications such as QuickBooks or Google assistant. These virtual assistants can be very helpful as they are able to track multiple items and can give you reminders at specific times.

5. Make a list of tasks you need to get completed. If there is one thing that I will never get tired of, it is writing a list. It helps me focus my mind and schedules my day out, so I know what exactly I need to focus on first. The workload in the office can seem daunting but writing a list every day before you go to bed is beneficial for you. It will help release any worries of uncompleted assignments you think you might forget, and it will give you a jumpstart to your day in the morning.

Not only will it keep you more organized, but it will boost your brainpower, too. According to Dr. Cynthia Green who wrote a guest post on the blog "The List Producer" is all about how list-making can save your brain, the simple act of creating a list uses part of your brain that you normally might not use. It will enhance it in ways that will benefit you and your workload. It's essentially a win-win.

6. Take a break, which may seem counterproductive, but for most Americans, we feel guilty taking breaks throughout our work shift. We sometimes feel if and when we do, we lose time during our day to complete the mountain-sized load of work. But it's really important to take that lunch break to keep sane and organized. In a "One Thing" article that references David Levitin, a neuroscientist, and author of "The Organized Mind", he states that taking a break allows one to daydream. Daydreaming frees your mind of any work impurities and transcends your mind to be more open and might give you a boost in production.

7. This one may sound dumb but keep your desk clean. An organized desk will look good and you will know where everything is, but on a bigger note, it will keep you completely organized with your mind and your things. According to an article on Forbes, a report by OfficeMax found that office clutter undermines productivity and motivation. "Your performance coincides with your workspace," said Dede. "When it's organized and precise you have the mindset and motivation to work." If you are stressing out about your desk, you can't really focus on the work that is in front of you. That is why a lot of freelancers have their own office space or go to coffee shops, to get their mind centered and away from the mess they may have at home or on their desk.

Chapter Summary/Key Takeaways

This chapter discussed how to stay organized and make the most of your time. Some takeaways I feel are most important are:

1. Go digital if you can

2. Use virtual assistants
3. Take breaks
4. Make a list of tasks you need to accomplish

The next chapter will discuss how to communicate with your clients effectively and gain the most out of your encounters.

Chapter Seven: Improving Client Communications

Client communications are important. Plain and simple, especially when you run a service-based business. Communication with your clients is incredibly important. Proper client communication keeps your company thriving.

If your client communications leave something to be desired. That typically means lost opportunities (fewer sales and follow-ups). These setbacks require more money for marketing, and they create an overall downward trend for revenue and profits. It doesn't have to be that way. It can be simple.

Here are a few tips to improve client communications and make your company even stronger.

Take Your Time

When getting ready to meet with a client (potential or longstanding), do your homework. For new or potential clients, do as much research about the client and their needs as possible until you are completely familiar.

If it is a longstanding client, review their file, and talk to anyone else in the company who may have dealt with them. For new and potential clients, consider giving them some "homework" to do.

Routine Client Communications

Develop a system of communications to help your clients keep your company at the forefront of their minds. Develop a plan that provides the information, most likely in email form, which helps them stay connected.

Send out sales and promotional information that might get them to come back in the door. Provide your clients with key information.

Consider having your sales team reach out to established clients after a certain period. It's when you expect they may need your company's services again. Be available for them!

Finally, use social media to keep your company and its services at the top of their news feed.

Add a Personal Touch

Don't underestimate the power of a personalized message when establishing and building a relationship. Whether it's a handwritten note thanking them for their business or an email with a link to an article you thought they'd find interesting or helpful. Small gestures go a long way.

80% of people say that brands are not tailored to their needs. In a world where some brands like Netflix and Amazon are doubling down on personalization, smaller brands must also commit to this growing consumer trend.

Amazon's Alexa "gets to know the customer." The more "she" learns, the easier it is for consumers to buy products. Analysts predict that in the near future, 25% of all searches will be made with voice searches. This disruptive change means that excitement and engagement will matter even more in the future since ordering online through voice assistants will be about the instant brand recall.

Thoughtfulness is key. You can't simply send a generic note with the client's name at the top since that will cause the note to lose its effect quickly. Similarly, sending an email with a link to a piece of content will seem ignorant.

However, a note or email that shows you're listening to what they want and are actively trying to help them will strengthen your relationship.

Expectations

If communication is lacking or poor, it's your fault; not your client's. And it usually boils down to failing to set expectations at the beginning of a project. Along with providing reasons for what you do and why you do it, it's also important to set parameters for what you expect from your client and when you expect it.

Remember that they probably haven't worked with someone like you before or if they have, the process may have been different. So, give them timelines and due dates. Tell them when you expect feedback and client homework. I make it a practice to not only go over expectations and timelines before the project begins but to remind my clients of the next step after each part of the process is checked off.

Chapter Summary/Key Takeaways

This chapter touched on improving your communications with clients. Some key points to take away are:

1. Expectations, making sure they are clear and understood.
2. Routine Communication set reminders and make sure you routinely follow up with customers to ensure everything is operating smoothly.
3. Personalize your messages and be thoughtful.

The next chapter we will go over promoting the business and the vast amount of options that you have at your disposal.

Chapter Eight: Promoting Your Business

Once your business is up and running, you need to start attracting clients and customers. You'll want to start with the basics by writing a unique selling proposition and creating a marketing plan. Then, explore as many small business marketing ideas as possible so you can decide how to promote your business most effectively.

A unique selling proposition is a statement that succinctly outlines how your business, product, or service is different from that of your competition. It identifies what makes your business the better choice, and why your target clients should choose you over the competition.

Your USP can be an effective tool that helps you focus your marketing goals and verify that every piece of marketing collateral you create successfully sets you apart from the competition. Your USP can also be an important part of your branding that makes your business memorable.

This four-step exercise will help you write a unique selling proposition for your company, new product, or service.

Go Back to the Basics

The first step of writing a USP requires that you take a step back and review some of the basics included in your mission statement, business plan, market analysis, and overall business goals.

Start by answering some preliminary questions that recap what your business is selling or offering, who you're selling or offering it to and why you're selling/offering it.

For example, a company that sells picture frames may compile and answer questions like this:

What products or services are you selling?

Picture Frames

Who is your target audience?

Individuals who need to hang or frame photos,

What does your business do well?

We provide quick, responsive service while making the purchasing process easy for our customers.

What is your most important customer-focused business goal?

Helping our customers get the frames they need quickly, easily, and at an affordable price.

Solve a Problem

The next step is to identify your target audience's problem and explain how your product or service solves that problem.

Our example company that sells picture frames may identify the potential customer's problem as not being able to easily get quality picture frames when needing them most urgently.

Identify the Differentiators

This step focuses on identifying what it is about your solution to your customer's problem that is different, or better than, the solution your competition offers. The value you identify here will be one of the primary reasons why your customers will choose you instead of a competitor.

The potential differentiators of our picture frame company may be that they offer sturdier, less expensive frames, complete packing solutions, same-day delivery, or exceptional customer service.

Make a Promise

This step combines the most important elements of the previous steps into a concise statement that embodies the value your company has to offer. Keep in mind that your USP essentially implies a promise or a pledge, you are making to your customers.

The picture frame company, for example, may create a USP that says simply, "Quality Picture Frames in 24 Hours," aimed toward their overwhelmed customers who are looking for the best frames and fast.

Once you have a working USP, it's always a good idea to sleep on it, run it by others in your company, or even create a focus group to measure the impact it has. It may take several tries, but once you hit the perfect USP, it can be an integral element of your marketing toolbox.

Marketing Plan

A marketing plan is an essential marketing tool for every small business. To create an effective plan, you'll need to ask yourself and answer such important questions as:

What do I want to accomplish and why?

What is my target market?

Who is my competition?

Consider these important questions and more before taking any other action.

How Will Your Marketing Plan Support Your Business Goals?

Before you begin developing your marketing plan, you need a clear and specific idea of what you want to accomplish. It is your marketing strategy, and it's directly related to your business goals and objectives. Your strategy outlines what you want to do, and the rest of the marketing plan provides details on how to do it.

For example, let's say one of your business goals is to expand your brick-and-mortar retail store into an e-commerce website. Your strategy for that goal could be to introduce your products to a new national market segment. You would then break down your strategy even further into short- and long-term objectives while defining your specific message. Delve into how a marketing strategy and a marketing plan work together.

If you don't have them already, create specific business goals with a business goal setting guide to get started. Also, make sure you are attaching a specific timeline to your goals, such as a 90-day plan. Having a time frame helps you create a more targeted and realistic marketing plan.

What Are You Trying to Accomplish, and Why?

Your mission statement addresses what are you trying to do and why you are doing it. You may have already created a mission statement as part of your business planning process. If so, add it to your marketing plan.

Your mission statement is the foundation of your marketing plan. Although it may not play a direct role in your marketing activities, the mission statement focuses on your business goals and helps you make sure that your marketing activities support the business's overall objectives. It's an effective tool to refer back to whenever you start to question if you are still on the right track.

If you haven't finalized your mission statement yet, do so now. A mission statement tutorial can help you to get started.

Who Are You Trying to Reach with Your Marketing Activities?

Your target market is the specific audience you want to reach with your products and services or the group you are trying to sell. The more details you include as you determine who is in your target market, the more targeted your marketing plan will be.

Take time to conduct market research so that you can identify:

Who makes up your target audience?

Where you can find them

What they value as important

What they are worried about

What they need right now

Create a sketch of the person or business; you would consider your ideal customer. This exercise helps you identify specifics about that customer as well as personalize your marketing messaging.

Who Are You Up Against, and Where Do You Rank?

One of the best ways to research your target market and prepare your marketing activities is to study your competition. Know who is out there selling what you are, especially if they are selling it to consumers who fit your ideal customer profile. Take a hard look at what your competitors are doing right, and what they may be doing wrong.

One way to conduct a competitive analysis is with a SWOT analysis, a strategic tool that evaluates a company's strengths, weaknesses, opportunities, and threats. Take time to measure the SWOT of your top competitors as well as your own business.

Conducting a thorough analysis of your competition will help you identify areas where you can beat the competition, fine-tune your niche market, and make sure you are prepared to address competitive challenges.

What Makes Your Business Unique?

Once you know what you're up against in the market, it's time to identify the approach that sets you apart from everyone else.

A unique selling proposition outlines how your business, products, or services differ from your competitions. The statement identifies what makes your business the better choice, and why your target clients should choose you over the competition.

A unique selling proposition tutorial can help craft a USP for your business.

What Will You Charge, and Why?

If you have a traditional business plan, you already have spent a great deal of time researching the best price point for your products and services. Now relate that pricing information to your marketing activities.

One highly important factor in determining how you will work your pricing strategy into your marketing message. In most cases, you want to be able to support your price points by providing your customers with a clear idea of the value and benefits they receive in return. A high-value proposition often leads a customer to make a purchase.

If you haven't identified your pricing perspective yet, review a pricing strategy primer to explore different approaches and consider how they may relate to your business.

How Will You Reach Your Target Market?

As a key element of the marketing mix, your promotional plan covers all of the communication that will take place with the consumer.

Your promotional plan should combine a variety of marketing activities and may include:

Advertising

Packaging

Public relations

Direct sales

Internet marketing

Sales promotions

Marketing materials

Other publicity efforts

Don't want to start with too many variations in your promotional plan. Select three to five specific activities to help you execute your marketing strategy.

For example, if one of your goals is to provide five free initial consultations within three months, your promotional plan may include focusing on targeted leads through a cold calling campaign, a social media outreach plan, and a direct mail campaign. You can get some idea on specific activities by browsing lists of 101 small business marketing ideas.

Complete this step at the same time as the next step since your budget affects the activities you can include.

How Much Money Will You Spend, and on What?

As you outline a promotional plan, you need to have a budget in place so that you know which activities you can afford. Unfortunately, most new small businesses have a limited budget when it comes to marketing, so creating a promotional plan that works with your available funds is vital.

You may have an annual marketing budget, but you should also break it down into separate monthly budgets so that you can track results and modify the promotional plan to focus on the activities that provide you with the biggest return on investment.

A marketing budget template from Entrepreneur.com and another template from Microsoft Office can get you started.

What Tasks Do You Need to Complete to Reach Your Marketing Goals?

Outlining exactly what you need to do and when an important part of your marketing plan is. This outline becomes the task list to guide you through every one of your promotional activities. Your action steps help you stay on track so that you can make consistent progress without having to re-create the wheel every time you're ready to take a step.

To formulate your marketing plan action list, follow the same process for managing your daily tasks. Take the end goal, and break it down into a series of single-step tasks that lead you to achieve your desired result

For example, if one of the activities outlined in your promotional plan is launching a direct mail campaign, your first few action steps may look like this:

Determine your budget for the campaign.

Clarify your objective for the campaign.

Determine the type of direct mail you will send.

Hire a designer or firm to create your collateral. Or get creative and design it yourself.

Write (or hire out) the copy for the direct mail piece.

Clarify the call to action.

Create a draft of the direct mail piece.

Your action list can take a number of different forms, as long as it's created in a way that supports progress. Each action item should also include a due date that works with the timeline you created for your marketing plan. Typically, the smaller the steps, the easier it will be for you to complete tasks and build momentum.

What Results Have You Achieved, and Where Can You Improve?

All of this work you've put into creating a marketing plan for your small business will be rendered useless if you can't track and measure the results. This step allows you to take your marketing plan from a one-time, static document and turn it into a plan that grows and develops with your business.

The way you track and measure your results depends on your particular type of marketing tactics. For example, online marketing can be tracked using analytics and other internet-based metrics, while tracking offline marketing methods requires a more manual approach. Google Analytics will be helpful for you.

In general, the more standardized your tracking system, the more relevant your results will be. By measuring your results, you will become much better at tailoring your marketing activities to focus on the areas where you will have the most success.

For some ideas on how to track your marketing results, read more about marketing metrics.

One universal small business goal is to sell the business's products and services. This is usually best accomplished by positioning the business in front of the target audience and offering something that solves a problem or that they can't refuse or find elsewhere.

To this end, one of the smartest things a small business owner can do for his or her business is taking the time to develop a small business marketing plan that will set them apart from the competition. A marketing plan clearly outlines how you will reach your ideal customers by effectively implementing your marketing strategy.

There are thousands of ways you can promote your small business. With the right mix of activities, you can identify and focus on the most effective marketing tactics for your small business. Here is a list of 100 small business marketing ideas to get you thinking about all of the different ways you can promote your business. This is just a list composed to give you ideas. Remember marketing at first does not have to be expensive, you can take the cost-effective route and focus on cheap or free marketing.

Marketing Planning

1. Update or create a marketing plan for your business.

2. Revisit or start your market research

3. Conduct a focus group.

4. Compose a unique selling proposition.

5. Refine your target audience and niche.

6. Expand your product and service offerings.

Marketing Materials

7. Update or create your business cards.

8. Make your business card stand out from the rest.

9. Create or update your brochure.

10. Create a digital version of your brochure for your website.

11. Explore a website redesign.

12. Get creative with promotional products and give them away at the next networking event you attend.

In-Person Networking

13. Write an elevator pitch.

14. Register for a conference.

15. Introduce yourself to other local business owners.

16. Plan a local business workshop.

17. Join your local chamber of commerce.

18. Rent a booth at a trade show.

Direct Mail

19. Launch a multipiece direct mail campaign.

20. Create multiple approaches, and split test your mailings to measure impact.

21. Include a clear and enticing call to action on every direct mail piece.

22. Use tear cards, inserts, props, and attention-getting envelopes to make an impact with your mailings.

23. Send past customers free samples and other incentives to regain their business.

Advertising

24. Advertise on the radio.

25. Advertise in the Yellow Pages.

26. Advertise on a billboard.

27. Use stickers or magnets to advertise on your car.

28. Advertise on a local cable TV station.

29. Advertise on Facebook.

30. Advertise on LinkedIn.

31. Buy ad space on a relevant website.

32. Use a sidewalk sign to promote your specials.

Social Media Marketing

33. Get started with social media for business.

34. Create a Facebook page.

35. Get a vanity URL or username for your Facebook page.

36. Create a Twitter account.

37. Reply or retweet someone else on Twitter.

38. Set up a foursquare account for your business.

39. List your business on Google Places.

40. Start a business blog.

41. Write blog posts on a regular basis – one a week or every two weeks.

42. Create an Instagram account.

43. Create a Groupon.

Internet Marketing

44. Start a Google AdWords pay-per-click campaign.

45. Start a Microsoft adCenter pay-per-click campaign.

46. Comment on a blog post.

47. Record a video blog post.

48. Upload a video to YouTube.

49. Check your online directory listings and get listed in desirable directories.

50. Set up Google Analytics on your website and blog.

51. Review and measure your Google Analytics statistics.

52. Register a new domain name for a marketing campaign or a new product or service.

53. Learn more about local search marketing.

54. Track your online reputation.

55. Sign up for the Help a Reporter Out (HARO) email list.

Email Marketing

56. Create an email opt-in on your website or blog.

57. Offer a free download or free gift to make people willing to add their email address to your list.

58. Send regular emails to your list.

59. Start a free monthly email newsletter.

60. Use A/B testing to measure the effectiveness of your email campaigns.

61. Perfect your email signature.

62. Add audio, video, and social sharing functionality to your emails.

Contests, Coupons, and Incentives

63. Start a contest.

64. Create a coupon.

65. Create a "frequent buyer" rewards program.

66. Start a client appreciation program.

67. Create a customer of the month program.

68. Give away a free sample.

69. Start an affiliate program.

Relationship Building

70. Send out a customer satisfaction survey to gain feedback.

71. Ask for referrals.

72. Make a referral.

73. Help promote or volunteer your time for a charity event.

74. Sponsor a local sports team.

75. Cross-promote your products and services with other local businesses.

76. Join a professional organization.

77. Plan your next holiday promotion.

78. Plan holiday gifts for your best customers.

79. Send birthday cards to your clients.

80. Approach a colleague about a collaboration.

81. Donate branded prizes for local fundraisers.

82. Become a mentor.

Content Marketing

83. Host a webinar.

84. Record a podcast.

85. Write a press release.

86. Submit your press release to various distribution channels.

87. Rewrite your sales copy with a storytelling spin.

88. Start writing a book.

Marketing Help

89. Hire a marketing consultant.

90. Hire a public relations professional.

91. Hire a professional copywriter.

92. Hire a search engine marketing firm.

93. Hire an intern to help with daily marketing tasks.

94. Hire a sales coach or salesperson.

Unique Marketing Ideas

95. Develop a Logo for the business.

96. Create a business mascot to help promote your brand.

97. Take a controversial stance on a hot industry topic.

98. Pay for wearable advertising.

99. Get a full-body branded paint job done on your company vehicle.

100. Sign up for online business training to revamp, expand and fine-tune all your marketable skills.

Now you have a few brand-new marketing ideas to try in your small business, get started on creating or fine-tuning your marketing plan.

Once you have completed these business activities, you will have all the most important bases covered. Keep in mind that success doesn't happen overnight. But use the plan you've created to consistently work on your business, and you will increase your chances of success.

"SUCCESS DOESN'T JUST FIND YOU, YOU HAVE TO GO OUT AND GET IT"

Success.com

Chapter summary/key takeaways

In this final chapter, we went over promoting your business. Some key points are:

1. Sticking with the basics,

2. Utilizing advertising to fullest potential

3. Making a promise to the clients and keeping it!

Thank you for taking the time to read this book. I hope it has answered all of your questions and provided you with the insight needed to start and grow your business. I wish you the best of luck in your future endeavors!

Epilogue

I want to thank you for purchasing this book. I truly pray that it was able to guide you and solve any problems or answer any questions that you may have had.

To summarize what you just read, make sure that you do your research beforehand. Hopefully, this was able to put you in the right direction, so you can start your own business.

Understand your and your businesses basic needs, this will allow you to gauge exactly what you need to accomplish and need to obtain to successfully launch your company.

Leadership, this is one of my favorite things. I take great pride in my leadership ability and the abilities I have been able to help others develop to make them a successful leader. Being a leader isn't just about being a boss or the owner of a company. It isn't ruling with an iron fist. It is about taking care of your people. Listening to them and helping them with their issues. If you can be a coach/teacher/mentor and provide them with stability in their work, it will help to carry over to their personal life.

Cutting costs to maximize profit. There are a lot of ways you can cut cost. Don't do what large companies do such as Kraft Heinz and just lay people off or let them go. If you cut people to deeply, you won't recover, and you'll leave a bad impression with customers and future employees. Look at all aspects of your business, from advertising costs, down to the soap you use in bathrooms. Save where you can.

Engage with Customers. Ask for feedback, understand you have room for improvement. Build a meaningful and useful brand. Package your product unique so it stands out.

Organization, a pretty simple concept to understand not as easy to actually implement. Anytime you can go digital for record keeping, you are usually better off. Use virtual assistants, calendars, memos, and anything else that will help you to stay organized.

Communicating with Clients/Customers. Listen to your customers. Take your time to understand their needs. Be personable and use personal touches for each one. This helps build a good rapport and relationship. Be the solution to their issues.

Promoting your business. Understand that there are so many ways to accomplish this goal. Websites, referrals, paid advertisements, social media and so much more. Society today is pretty much all connected through the internet, so a website is a must have and you can use a free service to design it yourself. Always carry business cards and hand them out frequently,

Acknowledgments

A big thank you to Louis Linsley, he has been a true mentor of mine and has been by my side the entire time. Also, a huge thank you to my wife Amanda, for supporting me and my business ventures and for believing in me. Thank you to my two sons, Scott and Collin, for being the reason I push myself past every limit and for giving me that extra drive to succeed.

About the Author

The author has held multiple positions of leadership and has successfully run several multi-million-dollar companies. During his early 20's he successfully obtained his degree in Criminal Justice graduating with highest honors. John currently runs his own Consulting Company, Brothers All Around Service LLC, which specializes in business development. John also offers financial services to individuals along with workplace benefits. You can check out his website at www.brothersallaroundservice.com. Subscribe to his blog page and keep updated on current business trends.

John resides in the Pittsburgh area with his wife and two kids. When not working, you can find John and his family taking various trips, enjoying the outdoors and riding his motorcycle. Please feel free to reach out to John and ask questions.

www.ingramcontent.com/pod-product-compliance
Lightning Source LLC
Chambersburg PA
CBHW030009190526
45157CB00014B/1764